THE
JUST BECAUSE CLUB
Your Personal Metaphysical
Fitness Trainer

Claude Needham Ph.D.

Gateways Books and Tapes, Nevada City, California

ISBN: 0-89556-073-9
© 2004 by Claude Needham
All Rights Reserved. Printed in the U.S.A.
Book design © iTRANSmedia

Published by GATEWAYS / IDHHB, INC.
PO Box 370, Nevada City, CA 95959
(800) 869-0658; (530) 477-8101
http://www.gatewaysbooksandtapes.com

Library of Congress Cataloging-in-Publication Data

Needham, Claude, 1951-
    Just Because Club : your personal metaphysical fitness trainer
/ Claude Needham. -- 1st ed.
      p. cm.
    ISBN 0-89556-073-9
    1. Spiritual life. 2. Games.   I. Title.
BL624.N42 2005
081--dc22
                    2005008377

TABLE OF CONTENTS

JUST BECAUSE CLUB

There is something both tantalizing and captivating about the notion that one day we may wake up to discover this was only a dream, to discover we had another waking life of which we were unaware until awakening from the dreaming. Many authors have used this idea very successfully as a plot element for science fiction books and movies. This is nothing new, long before Hollywood started using this idea to power blockbuster films, Tibetan shamen and Australian aborigines told the same tale.

What if all of this really was a video game or an elaborate dream?

Pondering "What if" is a very powerful tool. Einstein is reported to have developed the Theory of Special Relativity by conjecturing "what if two parallel lines could meet?" There are so many examples in science of startling discoveries made by those who asked "What if" then took the all important next step of checking it out. Reality is an experimental science. It does little good to amuse yourself and gain the admiration of monkeys by making cool and groovy conjectures. Asking a question means nothing unless you have the will and cunning necessary to look for answers.

"Check it out"—three powerful words. If you have the courage to go past blind acceptance of another's answer, and if you have the integrity to not give up your curiosity, then your wonder can take you into previously uncharted domains of your reality. How else do you think a baby comes to such amazing discoveries as the existence of feet—they check it out.

Pretend, hypothesize, experiment and see where it leads. In other words be a scientist—a real scientist. You will be pleasantly surprised at how incredibly far you can go. "What if we could like send a robot to Mars and move it around looking at stuff?" "What if we could eat the leaves of a strange Chinese tree and it would like cure some rare forms of leukemia?" "What if my computer was hooked up to a network of other computers around the world and they could send information back and forth through the phone lines?"

There are times in any endeavor (scientific or otherwise) when one doesn't have a suitably prepared explanation for one's actions that matches the current politically correct, properly phrased justification. Remember when you cut the hair on your dolly (or little brother) that glorious summer afternoon—just before an outraged adult asked "Why on earth are you ruining your doll (or little brother) by cutting his, her or its hair?" From the phrasing of the question and the tone of the adult, it was pretty obvious to most sufficiently cultured children that "just because" was not going to be an answer well received. In fact, one of the things that you are taught early on is: it is not okay to do much of anything unless you already have a pretty solid idea of what the outcome is going to be.

During the systematic acclimatization to the demands of the work force, wonder and courage are often removed from one's daily formula. They are not part of a healthy politically correct diet. Not to worry, if you are reading a book like this, you're probably the kind of person who doesn't mind walking outside the box—and perhaps you even have the courage to do something "just because." This book was written for you and those like you.

This book contains over a hundred activities/experiments. Why do we refer to these as both an activity and an experiment? Because they are. They are activities complete within themselves. And, they are also experiments worthy of observation, note taking, and further investigation.

The title of the book "Just Because Club" comes from the fact that many of these activities were presented to a special private group of students during the 1980s as a program of weekly experiments. That was then and this is now. Then the group was limited to a select group of one hundred invited participants. Now this material is being made available to anyone with the financial wherewithal to buy a paperback book and the courage to participate in some rather wacky, off-the-cuff, sometimes edgy, often inexplicable experiments. We call these experiments and those doing them the "Just Because Club."

Why call it the "Just Because Club?" Let's face it, none of us could justify in the face of cynicism or sarcasm why we were "messing" around with these experiments—and more importantly we did not wish to justify ourselves or prejudice our results with a script matching someone else's politically correct expectations. Twenty years ago our answer to the question "Why are you doing this stupid experiment?" was just because. And that, it turns out, is not a bad answer. Not only did it keep us from being put into the position of defending something we weren't interested in being forced to defend, it also allowed us the freedom to not jump to conclusions.

Not jumping to conclusions is a pretty good habit. So we encourage that in ourselves and in others. Notice the careful suggestion "not jump to a conclusion." Nothing was said about "don't come to a conclusion." Rather the suggestion is to "not to jump to a conclusion." Jump meaning to form a conclusion prematurely before the data is in. That's very different than never coming to a conclusion.

When we first ran the experiment called The Just Because Club it was a smashing success. We shared these experiments with others in workshops and online for several decades. Now that several schools have asked permission to use these materials as part of their standard curriculum, we feel it's time for the book.

This is that book.

Are we finally going to provide background, assessment, analysis, and pithy verbiage about what the heck one should expect from these experiments and what does it mean if (fill in the blank) happens? No. We have resisted the temptation to do so for these past 30 years and we intend to resist that urge during this book as well.

If I, or anyone else, were to tell you what to expect and what it all means we would first of all steal your delight in your own experimentation and second of all we would limit your results to ours. Therefore, within the covers of this book you shall find a bingy-bunch of experiments in the form of simple activities without addition of voluminous explanation and other expository pontification. Don't you just love the phrase "expository pontification?" I could talk on and on for hours about it, but that won't help—now will it? In this case, as in most others, it is best to follow the K.I.S.S. Principle. Keep It Simple Stupid.

This book is constructed of a sequence of activities—one activity after another after another. The order of these activities —is partly by accident and partly by design. If you feel the need to skip an activity for some reason, please make sure it's a good reason. Many of the later activities assume the completion of the earlier ones. Often one activity will build upon another leading to yet another. Not to worry, you'll figure it out fine as you go. And if you can't, don't hesitate to write us care of the publisher and we'll be happy either to be amused at your plight or to help in whatever fashion we can.

[Editor's note: In this book, it is expected that you will exercise your own common sense. We understand that common sense is not as common as it used to be. However, that does not diminish its importance. In fact, the sillier and more robotic those around you become the more you shall need to rely upon common sense. Consider this an admonishment to step away from the apathy and start taking some responsibility. If you don't exercise a little common sense to look out for your own interest, who will?]

GO TO A SUPERMARKET

Time your entrance into the store such that someone else triggers the door to open—so that if you had never existed the door would still have opened at that moment.

Walk up and down the aisles without touching anything. Then, to leave the store, time it so that someone else triggers the door to open.

If you should accidentally touch something—a person, a shopping cart or a product—select something cheap in the shop, buy it and leave through the checkout counter in the normal fashion.

Don't buy the thing you touch since it may be a person or a shopping cart or something incredibly expensive.

The intention is to not touch anything. If all goes well, you will have entered without causing the door to open, walked around the store without touching anything and left without causing the door to open.

Keep trying this until you complete it to your satisfaction. Should you wish you may send a copy of your journal report concerning the activity.

Notes: What surprised those of us monitoring the original Just Because Club experiment was the almost unanimous reports of success in entering the clairvoyant vision—also known as a Bardo state. Some of the individuals did not have the verbal background to recognize what had occurred. But, when they described the activity it became obvious that something quite profound had occurred for them. For me, the lesson was this: simple, but exact changes in what we do can act as transformational triggers.

GO TO A MUSEUM

Yes, go to a museum—a museum with art on the wall would be best.

Time your entrance so that someone else opens the door.

Spend two hours in the museum. You may wander, sit, pace, look at the walls, look at the floors, look at the people, even look at the architecture—do anything other than look at the art on the walls or the exhibits.

If you find yourself looking at any of the art, cross yourself in the following fashion.

Touch the bridge of your nose and say quietly "Spectacles."

Touch the area near...(where the zipper of your pants would be if you were wearing Levi jeans) and say "testicles."

Touch the area to the left of your heart and say "wallet."

Touch the area to the right of your heart and say "cigars."

Make this absolution each time you mess up and look at the art. Continue thus for two hours.

Notes: These experiments are almost guaranteed to thrust you into the clairvoyant vision of the awakened state—also known as "the Bardos." However, should you not be capable of behaving in a discreet manner you will be viewing the Bardos from the inside of a lunatic asylum. Chill and be cool. You are walking around in a public building and museums are not renowned for their tolerance of weirdos and crazies.

DON'T TOUCH ANYTHING

Spend one hour at your home (or apartment) without touching anything other than the floor. The floor is the one exception. If there is an emergency, of course break from the exercise and handle it. Don't be silly; use your common sense. Perform this activity until you have done it to your satisfaction.

In addition to whatever other results you may get from this exercise we find it to also be a good method to filter out those robotic, idiotic order following morons that really shouldn't be let off the K-Mart parking lot. If you are too silly to pick up a fire extinguisher and put out a stove fire "because you are following instructions to not touch anything" then perhaps the subsequent experiments are not for you. And besides if you aren't touching anything how did the stove fire start? Hopefully you didn't put a 30-minute cake in the oven just before starting this 60-minute exercise. See we are also calling upon your ability to do simple math—or your wit to ask for help from a friend who does do math when you need it.

During this and subsequent exercises you will be placed in situations which place you off the net—this means phone, text messaging, computer, and et cetera. Part of your experience will come from figuring a way to do this without causing problems or mishandling emergencies. So, be smart and use some common sense.

GET A QUESTION ANSWERED

Have or get a question. This could be a question you are currently working with, a question that you would like to work with, or a question that has been bugging you for a while. In any case it should be a question that is real to you and you care about finding an answer to.

Hand write the question on two pieces of paper.

Mail one copy to yourself and mail one copy to: "Just Because Club—Question," P.O. Box 370, Nevada City, CA 95959.

[Editor's note: since you will be mailing a copy of the question to the Just Because Club Headquarters it would be a good idea to not ask a question that you would mind seeing published in a newspaper—always use common sense.]

After the two letters are in the mail, buy a newspaper.

After you buy the newspaper go to the library.

Page one of the newspaper will contain the clue that will tell you which book stack/aisle to use.

Page three of the newspaper will contain the clue that will tell you which shelf in that aisle to use.

Page seven of the newspaper will contain the clue that will

tell you which book on that shelf in that aisle to use.

Page nine of the newspaper will contain the clue that will tell you which page in that book on that shelf in that aisle to turn to.

Turn to that page. This page will contain the answer to your question.

Make two photocopies of that answer-page and two photocopies of the title page of the book.

Mail one set to yourself.

Mail one set to:

"Just Because Club—Answer"

P.O. Box 370

Nevada City, CA 95959.

After you mail the photocopied "answer" page to yourself, wait.

When you get the question and answer letters, don't open them. Sit at your breakfast table (preferably on a sunny morning) and ask yourself the question "What is going on here? Just what is going on?"

Now open the "question" and "answer."

INTER-CHAMBER TRANS-PORTAL: DOORWAY

It is not unusual to carry the illusion that rooms are connected by a common floor and common ceiling; and, if we poke a hole in the wall between two rooms we assume one could peek through the hole and see from one room into the other. Two adjoining rooms are assumed without question to be part of the same house or apartment.

For this activity, get the very definite notion that adjoining rooms are chambers connected only by an inter-chamber trans-portal called a "doorway." Perhaps you've seen a sci-fi movie or television show in which characters step through a transport leaving one dimension to re-appear in another? Or, jump through a slipstream or wormhole only to end up in another part of the galaxy?

Savor the notion that doorways between rooms in your home are inter-chamber transporters and that the rooms themselves may be in totally separate spaces—perhaps even in different parts of the cosmos.

Once you get this notion working, amble about the house.

Wander from room to room pausing at each doorway to remind yourself that the doorway is a transport mechanism between separate domains. Try to sense the transport as you slip from room to room.

As you step through each doorway, be deliberate. Step through as if you are stepping through a force field.

Spend an hour wandering the house.

SPENDING TIME
IN THE KITCHEN

This activity is performed in the "kitchen" of your house or apartment. [If you happen to be homeless or living in the woods you'll need to modify the instructions slightly.]

For this activity you are going to spend three hours in the kitchen without eating or drinking. That's right three hours without eating a crumb or drinking a drop. During the said three hours you can do anything your integrity and ethic dictate with the exception of eating and/or drinking. Consume nothing, zero, zip, zilch—drink not, eat not. You may cook if you wish just don't taste the food while cooking and don't drink a single drop of water, tea, milk, gin or any other liquid.

This may seem like a long time to go without eating or drinking. Okay, if three hours is like too totally long do two hours instead. If two hours seems too long move along to another activity and just forget about this one. [Editor's note: if you have a medical condition which requires periodic consumption of food and/or drink then it is your responsibility to follow your doctor's advice. In this as in everything it is your job to exercise appropriate common sense and judgment.]

To begin the experiment stand at the kitchen doorway.

Get the "Inter-chamber trans-portal: Doorway" exercise working. When you are sensing the doorway into the kitchen as an inter-dimensional portal, step through the doorway. Step through the portal as if something profound but unknown was about to happen.

Spend three hours in the "kitchen."

When you leave the "kitchen" at the end of the three hours do it in the same deliberate fashion as you entered.

After you exit the "kitchen" say to yourself (out loud), "Well, that's that. This activity is complete."

BE IN AN EMPTY BATHTUB

Yep, that's the experiment. Be in an empty bathtub for one hour. You read correctly, sit or lay in a empty bathtub (sans water) for one hour. You may choose to do this with or without clothing. I find a bathtub can be quite chilly without the benefit of hot water. The choice is yours.

While you are lying in the tub ask yourself the following questions:

What is going on?

How did I get here?

What am I doing?

Keep asking these questions throughout the hour. At the end of the hour, get out of the tub, make yourself a nice cup of tea, sit and drink the tea. Maybe have a nice faerie-cake or cookie. [Editor's note: if you don't happen to be a tea drinker, then a nice glass of clear water will be fine—no coffee, no soda drinks, or alcohol of any sort.]

If you don't have a bathtub, a shower stall may be an adequate substitute.

If you don't have a bathtub, or a shower stall, you may try

lying under the bed.

If you don't have a bathtub, or a shower, or a bed to lie under, you may try sitting under a table.

If you don't have a bathtub, or a shower, or a bed, or a table, you may try sitting on top of a filing cabinet.

If you don't have a bathtub, or a shower, or a bed, or a table, or a filing cabinet, you can try sitting on a coffee table or other piece of furniture not usually used for sitting.

If you don't have a bathtub, or a shower, or a bed, or a table, or a filing cabinet, or a coffee table, or other piece of furniture not usually used for sitting, you can lay your chair down on the floor so that you can sit in the chair staring at the ceiling.

If you don't have a bathtub, or a shower, or a bed, or a table, or a filing cabinet, or a coffee table, or other piece of furniture not usually used for sitting, or a chair, then just skip this activity and move on to something better suited to life in an empty warehouse.

CREATE A LIST #1

Create a list of films that you would regret not having the opportunity to view during this lifetime. This is the kind of list that you would give to some cosmic scriptwriter on the off-chance that he or she would write your seeing these films into your life-script.

Typically, the films on your list will be films that you have already seen. If a film presents itself to your attention for inclusion in the list and you have not as yet had the opportunity to see the film but through some agency or other are confident that you really, really want to see it, then by all means add it to the list.

To get the idea of it, pretend you are at the beginning of your life. A Ms. God has asked you for a list of films you want to view during your life on Urth. You make the list of films and give it to Ms. God. This very same Ms. God will then assign a guardian angel the task of making sure that during your lifetime you have the opportunity to view the films on your list.

This list may take up to a year to complete. You should, however, have about 80% to 90% of the list prepared during the first few weeks. The remaining part of the list may come to you gradually through the course of conversation and other moments of not-expecting-it.

After adding a film to the list, check your local "Mom & Pop" video store to determine whether or not the film is available. If the film is "in-stock" then mark said film on your list with "IN." If the film is not available, mark said film with "NA." Turns out for many of us that many of the films we would regret not having an opportunity to view are not available.

Save your list for future reference. There will be future activities drawing upon this list.

POSTCARDS FROM HOME

This "Just Because" activity is a keystone—a leap if you will—into the next level of "Just Because" activities.

"Oh no!!" you ask, "Am I ready? What should I wear? Is this the right time, maybe I should wait for more favorable stars? Egads, do you think there will be a quiz?"

If you like, you may create of list of such questions that come to mind when confronted suddenly with the notion of making a leap. Do what you like with said list. We shan't be referring to it.

Here's the experimental activity....

Find camera shots, perspectives or viewpoints around the house that remind you of being dead wandering around in the Bardo. [Editor's note: the word "bardo" may be new to you. Don't freak, you will undoubtedly encounter more new words in the future. In this particular case it might be best to gather a temporary "working definition" of bardo and definitely not fixate or settle on a concrete dictionary type definition. Some good places to look are *The Tibetan Book of the Dead*, *The American Book of the Dead*, or perhaps a simple internet search.]

Please pay particular attention to the construction of the phrase: "remind you of being dead." We did not say "remind you of death" nor did we say "remind you of dying." We very specifically used the phrase "remind you of being dead."

There is a very big difference between dying and being dead, and a very big difference between "reminded of death" and "reminded of being dead wandering around in the bardo."

"Whoa, what's this reminded of being dead stuff?" I imagine you asking, "And, what is this Bardo thing they are always going on about?"

Individuals (not all, just the kind I tend to hang out with) have the experience of turning the corner, catching a glimpse of the hallway in just that right light, maybe at a certain time of the day, and bingo-bango something is different. The phrase "Toto, we're not in Kansas anymore" comes to mind in connection with this type of moment.

The question then becomes, "But is this what they are referring to?"

That is a good question.

The recommendation is to start with the activity and discover through the process of interactive game-play the answer to this question and perhaps much more.

Some folks are so intense about "not looking dumb" and "not running into closet-monsters without being prepared" that they can't learn through the process of trial and error. [Editor's note: We are not suggesting that you or anyone should run into closet-monsters unprepared. In fact, we're not really sure where we stand on the whole closet-monster issue in general. So if for some reason you feel an overwhelming compulsion to run into closet-monsters prepared or unprepared we don't really have an opinion on that.]

DEAF, DUMB, AND BLIND

Imagine that you are sitting inside the control room of a 10-story tall robot.

This robot is made in the image of a human with arms, legs, torso, head, neck, and all the rest.

Inside the head of the robot, in the area where the brain would normally be, is the control room.

In the eyes of the robot are cameras connected to television monitors on the wall of the control room.

The nose has a built in smell sensor that connects to the control room.

The tongue has taste detectors built-in which send signals to the control room where you sit.

In addition the ears have microphones connected to speakers in the control room.

The skin of the robot has special detectors which feed input from every part of the robot into the control room as well.

Basically you are sitting inside the control room of a huge robot deaf, dumb and blind to the outside world except for the input coming to you from this sensor array of cameras, microphones and other detectors.

The control room has been designed so that you don't see

the control room—you experience the input into the control room as if it is direct input. You don't see a monitor on the wall of the control room displaying the outside world—you see the outside world. You don't hear sound coming from a speaker on the wall of the control room relating sounds from the outside world. You hear the sounds as if they are coming directly from the outside world.

Even though you are sitting in a control room of this robot experiencing the world through third-party detectors and sensors you believe it is direct and immediate. You are basically enmeshed in a three-dimensional detector suit experiencing an outside world from inside the control room.

Entertain this notion. By this we don't mean serve the notion tea and cookies. Rather consider the idea as something truly possible rather than just something presented to you as a weird thing to think about. What if it were in fact true not just something proposed to you in a strange book?

Spend about ten minutes a day walking around inside this robot.

BEHIND THE TIME

After spending a few sessions performing the previous "Deaf, dumb, and blind" activity it may have occurred to you that since you are experiencing everything through sensors you are a fraction of a second behind what is really going on.

Yep. It takes time for a video signal to travel a camera cord into the television monitor. It takes time for the signal to travel from a microphone into the speaker. It also takes time for the taste, smell and touch sensors to send their respective signals into the control room.

Let's face it, all of the environmental data you get is just a little bit old. Okay, it is only a fraction of a second old. But, none-the-less, everything you experience in this control room is something that has already happened.

Everything you experience is slightly in the past.

From now on when you do the "Deaf, dumb, and blind" activity remind yourself that whatever you are experiencing is from the past.

CAPTURED MOMENTS

Get yourself a set of 3 by 5 cards and a pen.

Sit comfortably at a desk or table.

Wait in quiet expectation for moments in your life to present themselves to your "remembrance."

As each moment presents itself write it down on a 3 by 5 card—one to a card.

The time you fell on your face at the bus stop—write that on a card. The time you tried to make a special birthday wish—put that on another card. The time you lay on your back in the field staring up into the tree when suddenly the sky became the foreground and the branches the background—put that on yet another card.

Fill out anywhere from 100 to 500 cards. Later you may wish to include detail. For the moment any phrase that titles the moment and acts as a key to remind you of the moment for subsequent remembrance will be sufficient.

At the end of about an hour or two you should have a pile of 100 to 500 cards.

Wrap the stack of cards with a silk cloth or sheet of aluminum foil.

Place the cards in an appropriate place where they will not

be lost nor exposed to undue interference by nosy housemates.

For the sake of reference we shall call this stack of cards "Deck of Moments."

Échasses.

DECK OF MOMENTS— ADD A FACT

This activity/experiment will use the "Deck of Moments" prepared in the previous activity. Bring forth said deck of moments and set yourself up at a writing station—desk or table.

Lay the deck of moments face down on the surface.

Pick the top moment and turn it face up before you.

Read the existing title and text on the card.

Then add a fact about that moment.

This should be a simple fact. It happened on Tuesday. It was in the garage. The standard who, what, where, when, and how type of stuff.

After you finish with the whole Deck of Moments put it away as before.

CAPTURED MOMENTS— ADD AN EMOTIONAL DETAIL

Bring forth said "Deck of Moments" and set yourself up at a writing station—desk or table.

Lay the Deck of Moments face down on the surface.

Pick the top moment and turn it face up before you.

Read the existing title and text on the card.

Then add an emotional detail about that moment.

This should be something that you recall about the moment from your emotional self.

After you finish with the whole Deck of Moments put it away as before.

CAPTURED MOMENTS—
ADD A SENSING DETAIL

Bring forth said "Deck of Moments" and set yourself up at a writing station—desk or table.

Lay the deck of moments face down on the surface.

Pick the top moment and turn it face up before you.

Read the existing title and text on the card.

Then add a sensing detail about that moment.

This could be something such as my left hand was tingling, the cool breeze rustled the hairs on my arm, I had a metallic taste in my mouth, there was an odd buzzy feeling in my stomach.

These "sensed" details are not restricted to skin sensations, taste and/or smell. We have many other forms of sensing that don't seem to be related to the typical nerve impulses. Don't restrict your details. All we are looking for here is a distinction between facts and emotions previously addressed.

After you finish with the whole deck of moments put it away as before.

CAPTURED MOMENTS—
ADD A VISUAL DETAIL

Bring forth said "Deck of Moments" and set yourself up at a writing station—desk or table.

Lay the deck of moments face down on the surface.

Pick the top moment and turn it face up before you.

Read the existing title and text on the card.

Then add a visual detail about that moment.

These visual details can be general or extremely specific—just as long as they are visual and not emotional or sensing.

After you finish with the whole deck of moments put it away as before.

CAPTURED MOMENTS—
ADD A SMELL

Bring forth said "Deck of Moments" and set yourself up at a writing station—desk or table.

Lay the deck of moments face down on the surface.

Pick the top moment and turn it face up before you.

Read the existing title and text on the card.

Then add an olfactory (smell) detail about that moment.

Often we ignore smells when recalling events. That is unfortunate since smell is a potent key when it comes to memory.

After you finish with the whole deck of moments put it away as before.

CAPTURED MOMENTS— ADD A SOUND DETAIL

Bring forth said "Deck of Moments" and set yourself up at a writing station—desk or table.

Lay the deck of moments face down on the surface.

Pick the top moment and turn it face up before you.

Read the existing title and text on the card.

Then add a sound detail about that moment. By this we don't mean a detail that is solid. Rather something you heard.

After you finish with the whole Deck of Moments put it away as before.

CAPTURED MOMENTS—
A REVIEW

Bring forth said "Deck of Moments" and set yourself up at a writing station—desk or table.

Lay the deck of moments face down on the surface.

Pick the top moment and turn it face up before you.

Read the existing title and text on the card.

Now answer the following question:

Is the incident selected an episode with multiple actions and a duration, or is it a single moment—a time slice?

If the incident on the card is a single moment—a time slice—then put that card aside as "okay" and continue to the next moment in the deck.

If the incident is composed of multiple actions then select any single moment from the episode that best captures that thing about the incident that inspired you to include it in the first place. Now, write a new card for that extracted moment. Put the new card in the "okay" pile and put the multiple action card in a new pile we can call "Later for you pile."

Go through your stack of 3 by 5 cards until each incident has been filtered.

When you are done you should have one pile with "okay" cards that truly represent a single moment and another "Later for you pile" containing episodes composed of several moments connected into an incident.

Save the "later for you" cards for later. We may or may not ever come back to these cards.

Put the newly filtered "Deck of Moments" away.

CAPTURED MOMENTS—SPARKLING

Some moments in our lives sparkle and some moments are grey. Some moments are bright active moments full of attention and others fade into the run-of-the-mill ordinary blend of sameness. Some moments are part of the background barely noticeable and others stand out as vibrant peaks.

These moments of sparkle can be happy, sad, painful, or full of delight. The quality of the moment is not dependent upon the nature of the activity or your emotional response.

A sparkling moment sparkles because it sparkles. And it sparkles because it sparkles.

Bring forth your "Deck of Moments" and set yourself up at a writing station—desk or table.

Lay the deck of moments face down on the surface.

Pick the top moment and turn it face up before you.

Read the existing title and text on the card.

If, in your opinion, this is a sparkling moment put it into a pile called "Sparkling Moments" Otherwise put the moment into a secondary pile called "Moments not defined as Sparkling."

Go through your stack of 3 by 5 cards until each incident has been filtered.

When you are done you should have two piles: one pile of "Sparkling Moments" and another pile of "Moments not defined as Sparkling."

Put both piles away for future use.

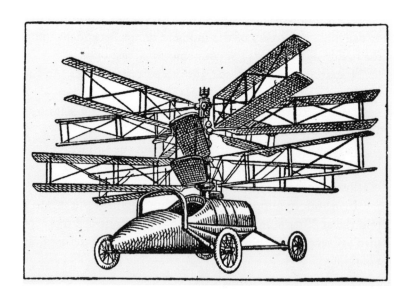

CAPTURED MOMENTS—AS ARTWORK

Bring forth the "Deck of Sparkling Moments."

Work your way through the deck from moment to moment. Whenever inspiration strikes and you feel inclined to do so create an art-piece.

Make a drawing, do a charcoal, create a pastel, paint in acrylics, create in Photoshop, or any other art medium. Whatever art mode you select the intention will be to make something which will capture the essential quality of the moment.

OUTSIDE LOOKING IN

Typically we have the perspective of being inside ourselves looking out at the rest of the world.

For the purposes of this activity/experiment we will assume another perspective—that of being outside looking back at ourselves.

To add an element of fun, we'll use a novel reminding factor for the activity—we'll wear our clothes inside-out. That means that each item of clothing is inside-out and the order of dress is reversed outermost first and innermost last.

For example, if you would normally be wearing pants and shirt over underwear and t-shirt, you would start dressing with your inside-out pants and shirt. Then layered over the top of your pants and shirt would be your underwear and inside-out t-shirt. Socks are easy enough to wear inside-out, shoes on the other hand a bit of a challenge. Lucky for you we recommend sitting in your living room or parlor for the duration of this activity.

The recommended time for this activity is an hour and a half.

Remind yourself periodically that you are outside looking back at yourself. Everything you see is your naked true self.

CARTOON PROPHECIES

For one week each morning refer to the funny pages of your local newspaper looking for the day's message.

It's not definite which comic strip will hold the day's key but it is certain that one of the comics will hold the day's message. This is not one of those "I guess that comic could be referring to me," or "I suppose if seen in a particular light the comic might have a message in it." No, the day's message will be obvious and direct.

It may require a little head tilting or shift in perspective on your part, but just like the picture of two faces that might be a vase or vase that might be two faces, when your attention clicks on the proper strip it will be clear.

If you find a message that is telling you to do "stuff," that is not the comic for the day. If you keep finding messages that contain instructions and directions for what to do please see your assigned counselor and have them up the dosage on your meds.

Because I believe the distinction is subtle yet profoundly important I'll include a little story:

Back in 1986 when I was first learning to sculpt professionally, I would leave one of my works in process conspicuously along the path my sculpture mentor would travel each morning on the way to his office—this being my not very subtle attempt to elicit a comment or two on my latest carving. My sculpture teacher was extremely sparse with comments. On this given morning I was rather hoping that I could prompt him into a more substantive comment since I'd hit a bit of a quandary with the piece in progress. Rather than tell me to change this or do that differently; rather than tell me anything specific about how to solve the carving, he just said "Be brave." The instant he said that I knew precisely what I needed to do on the piece. I had been subconsciously debating and wrestling with a possible solution all night long. The only thing holding me back was trepidation about drastically altering a piece that was virtually finished. I didn't know if I wanted to head back in with hammer and chisel on a piece in the final stages of sanding.

So the simple "Be brave" gave me the exact focus I needed to take action without actually indicating any specific steps.

I hope you see the difference.

The "cartoon prophecies" should operate the same way. They should be bang on enough to afford no doubt that they are meant for you, without indicating any specific actions.

[Editor's note: If the cartoon prophecies are telling you things like "Go knock over a gas station" or "Burn your shoes in a barbecue" please visit the county medical center and get some professional help.]

BAKE SOME COOKIES

Bake yourself a nice batch of chocolate chip cookies. If you don't have a preferred recipe—the chocolate chip bag from the cooking section of the grocery store has a fine recipe.

Oh, and yes there is one teeny, tiny little spin on the activity.

Pretend that you are living in a society that forbids prayer. In addition, pretend that this society has vid-cams all over the place watching every move you make just in case you might try to slip in a few words of prayer when no one is watching.

Not a problem for you, as you're a member of the Reformed Church of Later Afternoon Chocolate Chip Cookie Bakers. In this pretend society prayer is done through the invisible tradition of making cookies.

So go forth and pray—just be careful to not say or do anything that would be obviously religious as defined by the moronic PP (Prayer Police) who are watching your every move.

PEEK-A-BOO

Find a partner that won't mind an hour of utterly silly fun.
The two of you will take turns playing peek-a-boo.

Select who will go first. That person will be the one doing
peek-a-boo. The other will be the recipient.

In case you are new to the planet, here's a brief rundown of
one method of playing peek-a-boo.

After establishing visual contact with your partner, cover
your eyes with your two hands like closed curtains (or shutters
of a lens).

Then say "peek-a-boo" and open your hands to reveal yourself to the astonishment of your partner. It helps to have a surprised and/or excited look on your face. If you can whomp up
the mood of astonished wonder so much the better.

Do peek-a-boo for 10 minutes like this then switch roles.

Repeat the experiment back and forth until you have both
given and received three times. This should take an hour.

PEEK-A-BOO #2

This version of peek-a-boo is performed in a mirror.

First establish visual contact with yourself in the mirror. Then cover your eyes with your hands as in the previous experiment. Wait for the right time, then pull your hands apart to reveal yourself to yourself being sure to say peek-a-boo nice and strong.

Do this for fifteen minutes at a time. After doing a half dozen sessions of this you may choose to continue on a periodic basis, or you may choose to set the experiment aside. Your choice—after doing a half dozen fifteen minute sessions.

INSTANT REPLAY

Select a simple activity from your day such as washing dishes, vacuuming the carpet, making your bed, getting dressed in the morning, or....

Do the activity as usual.

Then right after finishing rewind and do it again.

Then right after finishing rewind and do it again.

Then right after finishing rewind and do it again.

Run the "instant replay" a total of 5 to 7 times.

[Editor's note: Obviously for this type of experiment feeding the dog would be a bad choice of activities to repeat. The poor thing would be way overfed by the time you've repeated 5 to 7 times. We're sure you can think of other activities that would be equally hard on yourself or others—don't use them either for this experiment.]

GIVE THAT TO ME AGAIN

This activity requires a partner.

Select a book such as Alice Through the Looking Glass or Huckleberry Finn.

Reader and listener sit comfortably across from each other in simple straight back chairs—no couch or recliners please. The knees of reader and listener should be about 12 inches distant. Sit with both feet flat on the floor.

The reader begins to read then at a random moment the listener will say "Give that to me again."

After the reader re-reads the entire line the listener will say "thank you" pause a brief moment and repeat "Give that to me again."

Repeat the line for 15 minutes to 30 minutes.

When the time has expired the listener should say "thank you, let's continue."

The reader will then continue reading aloud from the page until the page is complete.

After the page is complete, switch roles and repeat. Do this back and forth for an hour or two.

WAIT FOR THE RIGHT MOMENT

Begin this activity when you have an hour or two free of obligations.

Sit down in a comfortable straight back kitchen style chair.

Continue sitting until "the right moment" then get up and proceed with the rest of your day.

Don't get up just after the right moment, or just before the right moment. Get up at the right moment.

If you miss the right moment, wait a bit. Another will come along.

PUSHING HANDS WITH THE INEFFABLE

I'm most familiar with "pushing hands" from Tai Chi. You may have seen it in a kung fu movie or given the growing popularity of Tai Chi you may have practiced it yourself. If not, don't worry. We'll try giving you an explanation of the process; if that fails, then you can always find a local teacher or friend that can show you how it's done.

The principles of "pushing hands" are simple. When your opponent presses in toward you, you give like a willow in the wind. When your opponent gives, moving away from you, you press toward him/her like bamboo flexing toward the sky in the easing wind. The subtlety of pressure, the difference between advancing and retreating is minute—barely noticeable. This dance between opponents advancing and retreating is as intimate as touch-dancing or love-making—each anticipating the moves of the other and responding even before they become known.

In the case of "pushing hands with the ineffable" your opponent will be the invisible presence just one hair's breadth away.

So while this is a solo activity it's not done alone.

Put your arms and hands before you as-if counter to a traditional opponent.

Wait for the breath of pressure and respond appropriately by either advancing or retreating.

Do this for 15 minutes, 30 minutes, or an hour.

[Editor's note: as stated this is a solo activity, but it is possible to do with a room full of others also involved in the same solo activity.]

SWING YOUR ARMS SLOWLY

When walking it is quite natural for one's arms to swing at your sides. Walk around a bit and you'll notice this fact. You'll also notice that the swinging of the arms is in time with your steps.

For this activity/experiment deliberately swing your arms much slower than normal while you walk. It should take five to ten steps for your arms to swing through one cycle. This slow motion swing of your arms can be slowed even more should you wish.

BUSY ROOTS, SLOW PETALS

This activity/experiment is best done in a group of five or more—but, any size group from one to a hundred is fine.

Stand in a circle facing toward the center of the circle.

Stand with your arms relaxed at your sides.

Start tapping your feet (like running in place), one-two-three-four, one-two-three-four, one-two-three-four, etc.—so that each count of four steps requires about one second. This is a moderately fast pace.

While the feet are busy doing their thing, raise the arms slowly as if they are attached at the wrists by strings connected to balloons. Raise the arms until just over shoulder height then allow them to settle just as slowly. The rise and fall should take about ten seconds each—that means the hands will take about 20 seconds to complete one cycle of up and down movement while the feet will be tapping away in rapid four-four count.

The first few times you do this experiment do the movement part for three minutes on followed by a period of two minutes off. Repeat the cycle a half dozen times.

After working with this experiment for a few weeks, increase the time to five minutes on and two minutes off—five cycles.

Then finally ten minutes on with three minutes off for three cycles.

During the couple of minutes when not tapping the feet, the arms should rest quietly at the sides in a pose not unlike an English Royal Guardsman who refuses to twitch or move even though tormented by silly tourists.

I AM A CLONE

Let's assume for the sake of make-believe that cloning has been perfected. Along with cloning there's also been perfected a memory transfer process.

This means that each clone has the complete and exact memory, sense of history, and habits as the original.

As mentioned this is all part of make-believe. Continuing along that vein let's assume that somehow you've discovered that you are not the original you as you thought. Instead you are a clone.

Sit quietly absorbing this bit of news.

Remind yourself periodically as you sit pondering this situation "I am a clone. The memories, history, and habits that I believe are mine belong to the original. I am a clone."

CLONE-ANON SUPPORT GROUP

Each person in the meeting begins with "Hello, my name is (fill in the blank); I am a clone."

Then proceed to give some details about interesting, odd, ghastly, amazing, or wonder-inducing things you find yourself doing throughout the day as a result of the cloned conditioning.

"Apparently the alpha was an accountant because I persist in finding myself at an accounting firm each day doing financial reports.... The alpha must be fond of chocolate since every time I walk by a candy bar machine I have an as-if desire to buy and consume a chocolate bar, etc., etc."

The "alpha" is how we refer to the prototype from which you must have been cloned.

WALK-IN SUPPORT GROUP

Each person in the meeting begins with "Hello, my name is (fill in the blank); I am a walk-in."

Then proceed to give some details about your experience as a "walk-in" in that particular life. In case, you're not a fan of weird science fiction or weird science you might not know that a "walk-in" is the name given to a spiritual being that steps into a preexisting life. Showing up after the body, mind, and habits have already been through many years of development.

This is very similar to, but different than, the "Clone-Anon Support Group" activity. We recommend switching back and forth between the two types of group activities. The reason for this is simple. While for you this may be just a "Just Because Club" activity there are those for whom these ideas are real. By switching between the two we hope to avoid becoming identified with these notions as permanent philosophies. Get the drift.

WHICH PART IS NOT A CLONE

As you discovered in our make-believe activity/experiment "I am a clone" you may or may not be the original you.

Let's go on an expedition to discover that aspect of you which cannot be cloned.

We already know that memories, history, and habits can be transferred in the cloning process. So the question remains "which part of you is not able to be cloned? "

As a possibility arises ask yourself, "Is this something which is part of the cloneable machinery"—i.e., memory, body parts, and so on. If the item you're testing could be part of the cloneable machinery say to yourself "I am not that."

Keep looking for that which is you.

A SCENE FROM AN UNKNOWN PLAY

At the moment you are mostly likely reading this page. Or someone else is reading this page to you. The difference between you reading this page and an actor playing a scene in which reading this page is part of the action is the actor can remember a time before stepping onto the stage to play the scene.

What if your acting method was to immerse yourself into the character so much that you couldn't recall a time when you were not the character. You can't recall auditioning for the role. You can't recall rehearsing your part. You can't even recall standing off stage just a few moments ago before stepping out on cue.

Once a day (or whenever you think of it) play the scene in which you happen to find yourself with the knowledge that you are an actor playing a scene from an unknown play.

EAT BLUE FOOD

Blue is not a standard color for food. In fact it is not very likely that you can find any truly blue food. If you'd like, you can spin off into hours of conjecture on just why that is that there is little or no blue food. But that is not what this activity/experiment is about.

We don't really care at this particular moment why blue food is so avoided by humans of the planet Earth.

At this moment we are contemplating a rather outrageous activity/experiment— the consumption of blue food.

Yes, we aim to eat food that is blue. Since blue food is not naturally occurring we shall need to make it.

We've found blue food coloring an absolute necessity in this.

Mashed potatoes, yogurt, milk, cookies, bread, cream of wheat, and whatever you happen to create can be eaten blue.

Start by having a blue meal. Include as many blue items as you can.

Later consider having one blue meal a week.

[Author's note: I am aware of blueberries. Yes, they are sorta-blue. And even blue cheese has a sorta-blue quality. Apart from these few exceptions you must admit blue is a rather rare color for food.]

CONVERSATION IN THE RESTAURANT

Find yourself a crowded lunch restaurant or coffee shop. You're looking for one of those busy places with a zillion and one conversations all going on at the same time.

Get yourself a drink and newspaper—or other suitable camouflage. The idea is to look as if occupied.

Next listen to the conversation that is going on in the shop. Don't listen to conversations from adjoining tables. Nope, that's not the idea. Listen to the larger conversation that is happening. This conversation is composed of one word here and another word there—different voices from different tables contributing to the whole of the conversation.

At any point during the conversation that you wish to leave simply get up and exit. There is no time limit. If this is one of those places where you pay later be sure to pay before exiting. Otherwise you might be testing out the activity called "Being hauled in for running out on a check."

Speaking of inappropriate behavior, I'd like to mention yet again that these activities are primarily designed to exercise your essence and promote a being-vision of the world. A secondary benefit of these activities/experiments is the development of a cool-head common-sense manner in dealing with the extraordinary. If you have a tendency (or even a ninedency) for drama and melodrama it is best to simply return this book to the store for a refund. Otherwise you may end up being a non-voluntary visitor at your local home for the criminally bewildered. A shaman is someone that not only has the ability to see the world through the eyes of being, a shaman is also able to be appropriate to whatever space he or she happens to be in. Not a bad skill to develop.

Diabolo.

WHAT ARE THEY DOING NOW?

Create a short list of friends and family whom you see on a regular, or semi-regular basis. You can do this mentally or on paper. Choice is yours.

Now sitting in a comfortable chair with both feet on the floor and hands resting relaxed upon your thighs go through this list addressing the following question.

"What are they doing now?"

Get a clear mental picture of where they are and what they are doing.

Picture the environment—hear whatever there may be to hear, smell whatever there may be to smell. Get as clear an image of their circumstances as you can.

Do this for everyone on your list.

This is the kind of activity that can benefit from repetition. Perhaps once a day for a month?

FIND A ROCK

The title of this activity/experiment says it all—well, maybe not all but a lot.

The basic notion is to find a rock. But what kind of rock? What will it be used for? Will this count toward the final grade?

Let's ignore the last two questions and address the first. What kind of rock?

Since you need to carry the rock home perhaps a not-too-heavy rock would be a good idea.

Also, since you may end up carrying this rock in your pocket from time to time perhaps a rock without pointy bits and scratchy parts would be a good idea—also something that doesn't crumble might be nice.

And, given that you may store this rock on your alter area it may be a good idea if the rock doesn't stink and that it plays well with others.

LEAVE A THEATER

Go to an afternoon showing of a film. Select a movie that ends well before sundown.

Watch about one-third of the film then get up from your seat and leave the theater.

As you leave the theater pay particular attention to the experience. Pretend that later that day when you go home you're going to make a journal entry about "Leaving the Theater" and you want to remember as much of the experience as you can. Keep in mind, if you don't pay attention in the first place you can't expect to recall it later.

Now comes a special little bonus.

Typically when you enter a theater you have committed yourself to two and a half hours. That time would be gone, used, spent. Well, by leaving the movie you've just gained an hour and a half that you would not have had otherwise.

What have you been putting off "because you just don't have time?"

Buying a new pair of shoes, visiting the new library they built last decade, ????

Make a short list of things you have been putting off because they did not have priority. Now that you have an hour and a half given back to you invest it in one of those activities.

TURN THE TV UPSIDE DOWN

[Editor's note: Depending upon your model of television you may or may not be able to do this activity. Please don't do anything stupid that will harm your television or if you do please realize that just because the writer of this book does strange experiments and even goes so far as to relay the instructions by which he does them; that does not give you permission to dismiss your common sense. This goes for this activity/experiment and all of the activities within this book.]

Hi, it's me the author again. I'm not sure why the editor decided to get all warning and cautionary all of a sudden. Maybe they had a bad experience with television sets when they were young. In any case here's the instructions for this activity.

Turn your TV upside down.

There that's the instructions. Don't be misled by brevity. Read it a few times if you need more words.

Watch television in this position for a while, maybe a week.

Don't succumb to temptation to turn the set right-side-up for that all important soap-opera or whatever it is you consider important.

TURN OFF THE SOUND

Another fun thing you can do with the television is "turn off the sound."

Try it. You'll find more than "lip-reading" will come from the experience.

If performing this activity in a group, maintain absolute silence.

That fact that sound is not blaring from the television is not an invitation to chatter on. In fact, create within yourself the notion that the sound is still very much coming from the set. It's just that, somehow, the sound has slipped a groove and is not on the same reality track as you.

CREATE A NEWSPAPER FROM THE DATE OF YOUR BIRTH

This activity may take more than a few sessions. Create the front page of a newspaper from the date of your birth.

Start with headlines then add short articles.

If you need to do a little research, feel free. Just avoid direct copying of material.

Be playful and have a good time.

CREATE A NEWSPAPER FROM YOUR DEATH DATE

Without including any specific dates, create a newspaper front page from your death date.

If you think there may be a man walking on Mars put in such a headline. If the ozone hole has shifted course and is now burning its way toward Texas put in such a headline.

Whatever pops into that little head of yours is fair game.

BUY A USED BOOK

Hopefully you recall what books are and even have such a thing as a used-book store in your town. If your town does not have a used-book store then reserve this activity until visiting a town that does have such a store.

Enter the store.

As you enter the store repeat to yourself sub-vocally:

"I know I am looking for something.

I don't know what it is.

I just hope I recognize it when I find it."

Now wander the aisles looking for the book to buy. Not just any book. Find the book you are meant to buy today.

This is not an expedition to pick up that cookbook you've been meaning to buy. Nor is it an opportunity to buy the next book in that series you've enjoyed so much.

On this expedition your goal is the buy the book you are meant to buy.

Do that, then go home.

WHO LIVES HERE

Look around your study or bedroom asking the simple question "Who lives here?"

Do your best Sherlock Holmes deductive reasoning to unravel the mystery of who lives here.

What can you deduce from the surroundings?

What do the occupant's belongings tell you?

Gather evidence from the physical room and its possessions.

All conclusions you draw should be solely from the evidence around you. Don't start interjecting things you know, or think you know, about the person "who lives here," force fitting or pretending that the objects indicate such. Start with the room and draw evidence from there.

Whether doing this activity solo in your own room, or running this activity as part of a group function on someone else's room remember the words of Buckaroo Banzai: "You don't have to be mean."

Look as if there is some subtle revelation just a hair's breadth away that, once you see it, will give you the clue to working with this individual.

FIND SOMETHING YOU LOST

Trying to find something you lost is a rather common activity. The difference between this activity and just looking for something you lost is: in this case you don't necessarily know what it is you've lost.

So, in this activity you will look for something you lost without necessarily knowing what it is you've lost.

I was looking through my bookshelf the other day and found a book missing from a set. I'd totally forgotten that I'd lost the book. The fact that the book was missing had slipped my mind. So now I'm looking for that "something which I'd lost."

While looking place a portion of your attention on the activity of looking for something you've lost, and engage another portion of your attention in an effort to remind yourself of what it was you lost—a kind of pushing or pulling similar to what happens when you "try to recall something that is on the tip of your tongue."

MAKE A LIST OF LOST THINGS

In doing the activity "Find something you lost" it is not uncommon for a whole list of forgotten things to come streaming in. When I'm reminded that I've lost the book I'm suddenly reminded that I can't find my trunk key, then I'm reminded that I've lost the skateboard wheels, etc., etc.

Make a list of lost things that you've forgotten until this very moment when you hunt for them.

This list will be labeled "List of things I'd forgotten I lost."

LIFEBOAT

Find yourself a four by six carpet. Hoodwink a group of friends into playing along. Then strand yourselves on a lifeboat.

Admittedly the lifeboat is nothing more than a carpet in the middle of the floor, and you're not really stranded since you could get up and leave anytime you like.

But for the sake of this activity/experiment let's assume the carpet is a lifeboat surrounded by swirling inhospitable waters. Let's assume you can't just get up anytime you want. Enter the lifeboat and do whatever you like for two hours—sit, sing, talk, play games, pick lice for each other or ?????

[Editor's note: If you happen to have a real lifeboat left over from an "end of the millennium buying spree" don't hesitate to use a real lifeboat.]

TEA PARTY

For this activity you will need a diminutive tea set with small cups and saucers along with a small teapot. You can probably buy one at your local Toys-R-Us or other large toy store.

The next piece of the setting may be a little more difficult to obtain, that will be a small round child's table.

Make a nice pot of tea—the best you have in the house.

Prepare a few finger sandwiches or other hors d'oeuvre.

Invite three or four friends over and have a tea party.

Treat your surroundings as normal and continue with whatever conversation or interaction you'd normally have. If you'd normally talk politics when sitting to tea or coffee then do so now. If you'd normally catch up on personal news do that.

Whatever you'd do, just do that.

Continue as if nothing odd were occurring. Carry on in your best imitation of unruffled British fashion.

EXTRUDED FRIENDS

This might be fun to do at a dinner party. Doesn't matter where, the approach will be the same and can be applied to many different gatherings.

As you participate in the gathering get the definite sense that everyone including you is extruded from the floor into the room. It would be as if sticking fingers into a balloon or another such elastic membrane.

SEE THE NEGATIVE SPACE

I like doing this activity/experiment at dusk. And it is especially nice if there's a mini-forest or other natural setting that you can view.

Sit watching the light change in the trees as the sun goes down. At a certain point the tree limbs and leaves will go dark and the negative space between the branches will become prominent. Go with that perspective.

See the background as the thing and the things as background.

FANFARE

Select some small rather insignificant activity from your day. Perhaps feeding a pet, taking mail to the post office, or doing the dishes. Something that would normally be part of the daily grind is best.

Having selected an activity for one occasion, make this activity into a major production. If it's doing the dishes, then get the soap just the right temperature before adding it to the sink. Balance the hot and cold perfectly, spend hours (if you like) selecting just the right outfit for doing the dishes, launder the towels, clean the sponge, do everything necessary to make sure every aspect of the event will be perfect down to the smallest detail. Plan this the way a movie screen bride plans a wedding with all the fuss and muss.

You'll want to eat the perfect dinner before doing the dishes so that everything will be just right. And you'll definitely want to purchase a perfectly marvelous candle for the windowsill and egads, don't forget to wash the window and get the drapes or blinds cleaned. Do it all.

Good luck, and don't forget to mop and wax the floor. Can't have a dirty floor when doing dishes on this night.

ONE LEG AT A TIME

Study yourself as you dress. Watch with the same fascination and intensity that a mimic would use in preparing for a new impersonation.

Do you have any quirks, or cute nuances?

Do you have any trademark moves or shtick.

As you study yourself dressing make notes. Keep a record book as a scientist would for any field study.

When it comes to publication it's the details which count. "I get dressed with my right leg first." is just not enough detail. What does the face do while raising the leg? By the end of this study you will have more than one hundred separate observations.

SMILE

Any actress, model, or public personality can attest to this one simple fact: "a non-spontaneous smile is weird to do."

Sometimes the necessities of the moment require a smile. If the necessity is a natural one then a smile will automatically form without effort and with a weirdness factor of near zero.

However, on those occasions when the smile is calculated the lips seem to forget what to do and the face can't seem to decide if it wants to grimace or smile. Here the smile is definitely not effortless and the weirdness factor can go off the charts.

This activity/experiment is to learn to smile.

Don't worry about the weirdness factor. Allow the storm of sensations to echo through the body. Just take note and move along.

SIT STILL

This activity can be done anywhere, anywhen.

It is best if you sit in a comfortable straight-back kitchen type chair or adjusted office chair.

Place both feet flat on the floor at a comfortable distance apart. Now plant them. Don't move your feet an inch, a fraction of an inch or even a fraction of a fraction. Keep your feet perfectly still.

Place each hand on your thigh (right to right, left to left). They should be in a comfortable posture so that your arms hang without strain at your sides. Now plant them. Don't move your hands an inch, a fraction of an inch or even a fraction of a fraction. Keep your hands perfectly still.

Next look straight-ahead. Allow your head and neck to settle in to a comfortable posture. Now, hold your head still. Don't move it, wiggle it, stretch it, snargle it, miffle it, or anything it. Just keep it still.

As you sit you may find that your vision diffuses or goes into what we sometimes call "wide-angle vision." This is where you are focused on nothing in particular and everything in general. Often you'll find the peripheral vision is brought into play. If this occurs don't fight it. This is what you want. Different folks have different ways of achieving this "diffused vision." For some folks they try for "diffused vision," other folks relax their eyes and look toward an imaginary horizon far in the distance, other folks give equal weight of attention to each element in the visual field, and some folks have no idea what I just said. Whatever works for you is what you should do.

This is called "sitting still with diffused vision."

It is an excellent practice.

You can benefit from five minutes a day, or fifteen minutes a day.

Caïman.

HOW DID I GET HERE?

Ask yourself this question: "How did I get here?"

This does not mean, how did I walk into this room, or what taxi did I take, or what career decision brought me to this place in my life.

Nope, this has more to do with a Twilight Zone, Outer Limits, science fiction kind of realization that you are in fact here followed by a sincere question of how did I get here. This is sort of like suddenly waking up in a dream, knowing that it is a dream, knowing that your true original home is not here (wherever here is) and then wondering, "How did I get here?"

The more genuine surprise, wonder, and/or puzzlement that you can whomp up the better.

Try to peek through whatever threads you can find to locate an answer.

WAIT YOUR TURN

You may do this alone, but it can be excellent fun with a group.

Prepare a room by putting chairs or a bench against the wall.

Take a seat along the wall and wait for your number to be called.

Admittedly since you did not take a number when you entered the room, and there is no one there calling numbers, in the normal course of events it will be a long time before your number is called. Hence, a time limit might be a good idea.

Use a time limit of either fifteen minutes or an hour.

When performing this activity with a group of associates be sure to remain anonymous and don't talk. If it helps, picture a massive bureaucratic office. Somehow you intuit that it would not be good to be caught chattering idly with others.

Once the activity is over leave the room still maintaining the appearance of anonymous non-interaction. You can re-enter after all have made the proper stage exit to have tea and cookies or whatever. Just close the activity by exiting with proper stage presence.

You'll notice the phrase "maintaining the appearance of

anonymous non-interaction." It is allowed, as you wish, to maintain a strong inner sense of being connectedness with others present.

STAGE PRESENCE

Stage presence is something you either have or you don't have. That doesn't mean one can't develop stage presence. Quite the contrary, if you don't already have the knack for stage presence, it is expected for you to develop it asap.

The point is that having stage presence is like being pregnant, either you are or you aren't. There is no sorta pregnant, and there is no sorta stage presence.

To practice, stand by the door outside a room. This will be the "stage."

Get the very palpable sense of an invisible audience looking down through a transparent ceiling of the stage.

Step into the room (stage), perform an act of some sort, then leave—make certain to not drop your stage presence until you have completely left the room.

You can do things such as rearrange the magazines on the table, alphabetize the movies by the VCR, pretty much anything.

When done as a group be sure to have each actor enter the room alone and exit completely before the next actor takes a turn. Later as skill develops, two and three person "plays" can be incorporated.

Each "play" should be an act that on the surface would

appear to be totally ordinary—if not for the fact that you were performing it deliberately for the invisible audience looking down from around the ceiling like a great tribunal gathered about the stage in the round.

WAIT FOR SOMEONE TO ENTER

Prepare the room by setting a chair in the center of the room facing the door. [If there is only one door in the room so much the better.]

The window drapes or blinds should be drawn shut.

Set the door so that it is open a fraction of an inch. It should be unlatched and open without allowing one to see into the adjoining room or hallway.

Contrive to run this activity/experiment at a time that no one is likely to enter the room. If you can be alone in the house or apartment so much the better.

Now, sit in the chair and wait for someone to enter.

BUY A TOY

Go to the toy store and buy a toy.

That's it.

There is more, but that is in the next activity. And it is most definitely suggested that you do this before reading ahead. Ooooo. That's a bummer. Now that it's been suggested not to read ahead, that could easily become the all important, over-powering necessity of the moment, which if it is not satisfied immediately might lead to the annihilation of life as we know it, or at least a deep nagging sensation of unresolved desire.

Try to bear through the pain and buy the toy before reading ahead.

PLAY WITH THE TOY

Hopefully the toy is still in its wrapper or bubble packaging—however it comes from the store.

Unwrap the toy and bring it forth to play with.

Intentionally have zero knowledge or assumption about what the toy is and how it is used. Make it be that this is the first time ever you have seen such a toy.

This assumption of zero foreknowledge about this toy is not make-believe or pretend. Rather it is an acknowledgment that everything you know, think you know, read, or have been told about this toy is either limited in scope or absolutely misleading.

Gaze upon this bit of creation with wonder and awe. Marvel in the mysteries which are about to be revealed to you for the very first time.

Now, go for it.

Play with your new toy.

WATCH THE GRASS GROW

If you have a rocking chair on the front porch so much the better. If not, prepare a comfortable place to sit and watch the grass grow. If you don't have a lawn, then obviously you'll need to mosey on down to the park or some public setting that has bench and lawn.

Sit and watch the grass grow.

Focus not on individual blades of grass. Focus, rather, on the whole of the lawn as one large vibrant being growing moment by moment.

ONE THOUSAND

In the various spiritual disciplines a thousand is not an uncommon number. Perhaps you recall "A Thousand and One Arabian Nights?" Yes, that is a collection of teaching stories.

Or, perhaps you've had the experience of asking a teacher what the effect of a given exercise will be, or what the bardos are really like. All too often the answer is "Do the exercise a thousand times then ask me the question."

Apart from being a convenient method of putting off pesky questions, perhaps there is something about actually trying something a thousand times which more or less guarantees you will have sufficient personal experience to either answer the question yourself or have the background to properly understand an answer given.

All that aside, what is it like to do something a thousand times?

Remember the rock that you should have found in a previous activity. In fact I believe the name of the activity was "Find a rock." Yep, that was the name all right.

Well, go get that rock.

Using a mat to protect the table and respect the rock, place the rock on a table in front of you. Place the rock at a comfortable position so that you can reach out and touch the rock without strain or stress.

Now, touch that rock one thousand times.

TOUCH A ROCK

This is an extra credit activity. (Or, perhaps a shameless plug for an amazing product developed by a work buddy of mine.)

If you caught glimpses of another world available through the simple act of touching a rock, then I strongly recommend you obtain a copy of *Zen Basics* (available from my publisher, GatewaysBooksandTapes.com, or http://www.zenbasics.com).

Zen Basics is heralded by Zen masters and shamen alike as a tool for meditation, ghost walking, and even preparation for the after-life bardos.

Mention you heard about *Zen Basics* through this book. Tell them the author says you should get a discount since you're a member of the "Just Because Club."

Let me know if they go for it.

SIT IN A CLOSET

Find yourself a convenient closet and sit in it.
Keep the door shut.
Keep the light out.
Sit on the floor of the closet for about an hour.
During the hour, sitting in the dark, on the floor in the closet, say to yourself: "If I were to open the door right now, I can't be sure what would be on the other side."

NEXT FLOOR

Use the same closet from the previous activity/experiment.
This time stand just inside the door to the closet.
Close the door.
Close the door with quiet certainty, not too fast, not too slow.
Pause for a moment, collect and ready yourself, then open the door.
Open the door in a smooth, even motion until you can see clearly into the adjoining room.
Use every bit of attention and discernment at your disposal to determine if that is the exact same room you left a moment ago.
Close the door.
Pause for a moment, collect and ready yourself, then open the door.
Open the door in a smooth, even motion until you can see clearly into the adjoining room.
Use every bit of attention and discernment at your disposal to determine if that is the exact same room you left a moment ago.
Close the door.

Pause for a moment, collect and ready yourself, then open the door.

Open the door in a smooth, even motion until you can see clearly into the adjoining room.

Use every bit of attention and discernment at your disposal to determine if that is the exact same room you left a moment ago.

Get the idea?

Repeat this cycle for an hour.

ACTS OF RANDOM GRATITUDE

Throughout the day, when you happen to think of it, have an overwhelming sense of gratitude.

For example, if you ask someone at the dinner table to pass the bread (and, you happen to remember this random gratitude activity) become extremely grateful for the bread, the fact that it exists, or the fact that you happen to be in a circumstance such that you can afford to have bread, or maybe because another being at the table was gracious enough to actually comply with your simple request. We'll leave the apparent reason for the gratitude to you. Just be grateful.

Your goal is to do this three times a day.

You may, if you wish, do it as often as you think of it.

Or, you may do it three times then call it quits for the day. That's up to you.

JUSTIFY YOURSELF TO A GROUP OF VEGETABLES

Prepare the activity by placing a group of vegetables—raw and uncut on the table or desktop.

Sit across from the vegetables in a kind of panel setting. [Editor's note: this could be similar to a board of review, JAG hearing, or dissertation defense.]

Address, with the vegetables, the question "What have you done with the life you've been given?"

Notes on vegetable selection: Everyone knows that vegetables can be implacable and often turnips and radishes can be judgmental. Because of this I recommend a jury composed of a wide variety of vegetables. A head of lettuce and zucchini may add balance to the group. But don't be afraid to include a few roots—carrots are quite compassionate and onions thoughtful and slow to reach conclusion.

YOU NEVER KNOW WHO YOU'RE TALKING TO

Preparation is simple. Just find yourself a place where others talk to others that affords you the chance to watch idly by without appearing unduly weird. For example, the park or a restaurant may work well.

Select a conversation from among those in your vicinity.

When we are reminded, it is obvious that each person in the conversation may well relay something said to another, and that other may relay the conversation to yet another, and that other to another in waves of expanding participation. Picture these folks standing behind and to the side of each person in the conversation.

Now instead of two talking we have two crowds of invisible proxies witnessing each simple conversation.

I'm not suggesting you should pass any judgment (for or against) this type of pass-along communication. Rather, just hold a mood of impartiality while you mull over the notion that one never knows who one's talking to.

Note: When visualizing this chain of influence be aware that talking is not the only means of communication—moods and experiences may pass along from one to the other without benefit of gossip.

ROLL THE DICE

This is a good activity for those occasions when you are in the mood for an adventure. This is also a good activity for those occasions when you are not in the mood for an adventure. It sort of creates itself.

Go on a walking tour of downtown. Each time you come to an intersection roll a six-sided die to determine which way to go.

1 or 6 = go straight

2 = go right

3 = go back the way you came

4 = go left

5 = enter a nearby shop and have a look about. Spend about five minutes before leaving and continue with your walk.

YOU NEVER KNOW
WHAT'S GOING ON

After doing "Roll the dice" a few times, you can add this activity into that mix.

Whenever you enter a shop (from the roll of a five) as you pass through the doorway into the shop say to yourself something along the lines of: "Based upon the appearance of this shop I think I know what's happening here, but really one never knows what's going on."

Apart from the obvious possibilities suggested by a large diet of suspense and action films, there are other deeper and less apparent alternate agendas in any given space. If it walks like a duck, quacks like a duck, and swims like a duck that doesn't mean you are in a pet store.

GIVE UP CONTROL

Don't freak. Even though this activity is called "give up control" we're not going to challenge you with instant chaos—why heck darn, the bardos do that for you each moment.

In the morning make a list of the top six things you must get done during the day. On this list should not be things such as "eat lunch" or "take the kids to school." Put on this list important but time free tasks. For example, "write a thank you note to Aunt Susie," or "clean out the fire place," or "shop for a new shirt," or.... You get the idea.

Take this list of six tasks numbered one through six.

Grab your six-sided die from the previous activity, and roll numbers.

The first number you roll is the number of the activity you will do first. That means if you roll a five first then the fifth task on your list is to be done first.

Keep rolling the die until all of the tasks are put into order.

Now given this sequenced list of tasks, do them—and do them in the order assigned by the dice.

GIVE UP THE REMOTE CONTROL

Now you may freak.

In this activity we invite you to give the television remote control to anyone with a penchant to surf the channels. The less his or her taste in viewing is like yours so much the better.

Sit without grumbling, harrumphing, suggesting, whining, snorting, or any other pseudo-form of communication. Your job is to "not have the remote control." So don't try running the one who does have it.

SURF WITHOUT CONSIDERATION

This activity works well with the one just before.

Assume the remote control and surf.

Go wherever you please, go wherever you don't please.

Switch channels when you want, switch channels when you don't want.

There are no rules about when and how often you change the channel.

The only rule is don't apologize or explain your choices and non-choices.

YOU NEVER KNOW
WHERE YOU ARE

In something like the ebb and flow of the ocean we slip in and out of proximity to otherness—places very much like where we think we are, only different.

For the duration of about fifteen minutes (or an hour if you prefer) say to yourself whenever the notion strikes: "This looks like where I think I am, but where am I really?"

WALKING IN A
PHOTOGRAPH

This activity is best performed in a quiet setting—no hustle and bustle. A few possibilities to give you the idea: weeding a flower-bed in your yard, sitting in your living-room, waxing your car, hand-stitching a quilt, washing dishes—basically anywhere such that you are the only moving part.

As you continue doing whatever it is you have chosen to do during this activity/experiment, cast your attention and awareness around the scene and suggest to yourself that you've been projected into a photograph.

ASPHALT BELOW ME

I give you this "Just Because" activity with a couple of cautions. One, do not do this activity if you are driving—do it when riding as a passenger. Two, if you are overly sensitive to motion sickness maybe it would be best to ignore this little experiment.

That said here's the activity:

Get the notion that you are sitting in a stationary vehicle suspended a few inches above the ground and that the asphalt is moving underneath.

TWINS

To prepare for this activity find yourself a portable or semi-portable mirror about 16" x 20" or larger.

Situate the mirror so that you may sit in a chair and look into the mirror seeing your reflection.

Get the notion that you are sitting face to face with your twin or doppleganger.

Empty the tension from your face, defuse your vision, and sit relaxed looking into the face of your "twin."

As you sit phenomena may occur. Don't pay it any particular attention. Just sit in "simple presence."

BE THE GHOST

Have you ever been a little creeped out thinking there may be a ghost or spirit running about the house? If so, this little activity just might get you through a few rough spots.

This activity/experiment is best performed sometime between the hours of midnight and 4 a.m.

Find a nice corner in one of the rooms of the house. Leave all the lights out—the same as if you've gone to bed.

Stand in the corner shoulders against the walls, watch and wait.

You be the ghost.

You be the spirit haunting the house.

You may wait for unsuspecting humans entering your house, or just hang around all ghost like.

Haunt your house from this corner of the room for an hour.

KINDRED MOMENTS

Remember the "Deck of Sparkling Moments?"

Well, bring the "Deck of Sparkling Moments" forth from it safe keeping.

Randomly select a moment from this deck.

Copy down the notes onto a pad or 3 x 5 card that you can carry with you throughout the day without putting the original moment at risk of being lost.

As you traverse the day, stay on the lookout for the moment which comes closest to this selected moment.

Each moment in your "Deck of Sparkling Moments" is composed of mood, sight, sound, thought, feeling, and more. As you look for the closest or most congruent moment during the day try to take all of these factors into account. Just because the original moment happened in a coffee shop and you are spending the day miles away from anything resembling a coffee shop shouldn't matter. The moods, thoughts, feelings and more can overlap without matching of the visuals.

Please note that in this activity/experiment you are looking for the closest moment not the most exact. If the matching moment you find during the day is more than a bit off from the original that's okay. We are just looking for the closest.

As time permits work your way through the complete set of "Deck of Sparkling Moments"—one per day.

WEAK SPOTS IN TIME

In addition to any direct results, the "Kindred Moments" activity may have a side-effect—noticing of weak spots in time.

"Weak spots in time" is just a phrase of convenience to refer to those occasions throughout the day when the boundary between present time and a moment in the past is a littler weaker than usual.

When these weak spots occur and why they occur is not our concern. Suffice it to say they do occur on occasion.

I remember quite vividly a moment in 1986 standing in my kitchen sanding a wood sculpture while listening to an "oldie but goodie" on the radio. (Yes, I was sculpting in wood at the time; and no, wood chips in the soup was not impossible.)This moment was well-connected with a moment in 1968. I even remember thinking in 1968 how odd that moment was then. I was sitting on my high-school bus riding in the morning to school listening to the same song.

It is not uncommon for two moments connected by a "weak spot in time" to share one or more common elements. Perhaps a song, a smell, an activity, a setting, or any number of things. There are no exclusive rules on what will and will not contribute. In any case that is not for us to worry about at this point. This activity is not directed to unraveling the physics of the process—just locating those few moments throughout the day when there may be weak spots.

PLEASANT COMPANY

From among your group of family and friends select some-one who is somewhat tolerant of your odd activities and is not opposed to a little experimentation from time to time.

Invite this individual to sit with you for an hour. This is a long time for most people and impossible for many. But if you keep looking you may well find a friend or acquaintance up to the challenge.

You can sit facing each other, or sit facing the same direc-tion, or sit facing opposite directions. In this activity, the direc-tion you sit doesn't matter.

Admittedly this sitting in the company of another is most likely something you've done before. There are, however, a few significant details which may be a little different:

1) Sit without fidgeting. No squirming, or wiggling about.

2) No talking, whispering or otherwise.

3) Position a screen or closed door between you and the one you are sitting with.

SITTING BACK TO BACK

This activity is very much like the previous—only completely different.

Rather than sit with a closed door or screen between you
and your fellow volunteer, sit back-to-back.

Sit about twelve inches (or a foot) apart.

Sit for an hour, no fidgeting, squirming, wiggling about,
talking, whispering or otherwise.

[Author's note: this activity, like many others, has a time
requirement. If you repeat an activity feel free to modify the
time requirements. However, you should do yourself the service
of performing the activity for the recommended time allotted—
at least during your first go at the activity. It has not escaped our
attention that for some people, and in some circumstances,
these times either are (or seem to be) long. But before you jump
to the conclusion that I am unreasonable in suggesting you sit
with a friend for an hour, please take note of the fact that if you
go to a movie with a friend you are in fact sitting with that person for something like two hours. So if it is possible to sit with
a friend for two hours in a movie theater, perhaps it is possible
to sit with a friend for one hour at home.]

CHERRY COKE

Find an ice cream shop.

Enter the shop.

Wait your turn.

Ask if they sell Cherry Coke—a Coke with a cherry in it.

If they do, thank them for the information and then do whatever. Get a coke, don't get a coke.

Leave instantly or loiter—doesn't matter. This shop will not work for our activity.

Keep looking until you find an ice cream shop that does not or will not sell you a Cherry Coke.

Next comes the critical question: "Can I get an ice cream sundae with whip cream and a cherry?"

If the answer is yes, we've found the shop we are looking for.

Order a plain coke.

Order an ice cream sundae with whipped cream and a cherry on top—any flavor of ice cream you like.

Pay for your coke and sundae.

Take the cherry from the sundae and put it into your coke.

Leave the shop with the sundae still sitting at your table uneaten—not even a taste of the whipped cream. If you must, promise yourself a very nice ice cream sundae from a different shop later in the day. Just don't eat that particular sundae.

Walk from the shop triumphant with your Cherry Coke.

SHUGUGLIO

Select a time.

Select a place.

Go to the place at that time and don't do any "Just Because" activities or experiments.

Do whatever is normal and appropriate for that place and time with one small proviso: don't get lost. Simply don't lose yourself in the momentum of whatever it is one does at that time and place.

FINISH WRITING A BOOK

Take an hour—no more, no less—and write the ending of your book.

At first blush this might be a little odd since you haven't written the beginning nor the middle. Don't let that stop you. Write the last paragraph of your book. If you are one of those rare individuals who happens to have written a beginning and middle of a book, then write the end of a different book.

DESSERT FIRST

Speaking of finishing things you haven't begun, how about eating dessert first?

No big deal, you're an adult. You can eat dessert first if you want. Exercise this odd freedom. One day for lunch or dinner, have dessert first, then the soup, salad and main course.

Suppress the desire to explain this behavior to fellow eaters or attendants. If you must say something simply express: "I'm an adult, I can eat dessert first if I wish."

Don't suggest it is part of some "growth" experiment (especially since we've never promised any growth benefits, psychological or otherwise).

Don't suggest it is for any dietary reasons.

Just do it as if it is the most natural thing in the world.

SIT IN A BOX

Find yourself a nice box large enough to sit in comfortably. Sit in the box.

Where? Your choice. You can sit in the box in the living room. You can sit in a box in the bathroom, you can sit in a box in the kitchen, you can sit in a box in the back yard, you can sit in a box at the beach. The choice is yours.

How long? An hour would be good.

How many times? It would be good to do this in a half dozen different settings.

If doing this activity with a group do whatever you'd normally do—except for the fact that everyone will be sitting in a box.

HOUSE OF CARDS

Using as many decks of playing cards as you wish construct a "house of cards"— just like the one you made as a kid. If you didn't make any as a kid then you are in for a double treat.

As you add each card say to yourself—out loud or sub-vocally—"I had nothing but myself with which to make the world, out of myself the world was made."

WATCH A MOVIE

I highly recommend selecting either *Buckaroo Banzai Across the Eighth Dimension, Rustler's Rhapsody*, or one of the many Marx Brother's films. If you select any other film we take no responsibility for the results. But then again, we take no responsibility for the results in any case. Still we recommend one of the above-mentioned films for this experiment/activity. If you can't find any of these, let us know and we'll try a different recommendation.

Now that you've selected a film, view it—once a day for one month.

Yep, you read correctly. View the film morning, evening, or night—just be sure you view it once each 24 hour period.

MAKE A FLIP-BOOK

Hopefully you've seen a "flip-book." If not, then do an internet search, such as on Google.com, for flip book and read up on the subject. If you've never seen or made a flip book follow the directions on the PBS or other kids' websites to create one.

Given some familiarity with flip-books let's move on to the core of this activity.

Select a quirk or mannerism that is sufficiently characteristic of you that anyone viewing a flip-book of that quirk will immediately guess it's about you.

Make a flip-book for that quirk.

THANK YOU
MAGIC SKUNK

In this world of automation and electronic gizmos of one sort or other, there are things that happen for our benefit without our direct participation.

For example, in some of the newer model cars the door locks will automatically latch a few seconds after starting to drive. Some of the odd new toilets will flush automatically after you finish. Or, perhaps you've noticed that elevator doors will close automatically behind you.

Select something from your life. Select something that is done for you for your benefit by one of these invisible helpers.

From now on whenever that something is done for you simply say: "Thank you Magic Skunk"—thereby expressing your gratitude for this help rendered.

FEED THE DUCKS

Find a place in your area where it's possible to take a bag of bread crumbs and feed the birds.

Venture forth with a bag of appropriate food—stale bread is often a good choice.

Feed the birds.

While tossing the food for the birds to eat ask yourself with some intention, "How do I receive that which is given to me?"

JUST SAY "YES"

For the course of one day, say "yes" to anything asked of you—with the stipulation that it does not conflict with your ethics or integrity. Have some common sense, don't say yes to robbing a bank, or anything of any sort that is sure to be a problem. If your children ask you to take them to Disneyland, that's a little outside the scope of this activity. If your parents ask you to cut your hair and burn your clothes ala "Pleasantville" that's a little outside the scope of this activity.

However, should you be asked to do something which falls within the bounds of common sense and does not conflict with your ethics or lawful behavior then do it. Just say "Yes."

GIVE WITHOUT REGARD

During the day, as you come upon gum-ball machines, insert a coin, turn the crank, then simply walk away—don't collect the gum-ball. If you are being watched go ahead and fiddle with the gum-ball release tray as-if you have the gum-ball.

STORYBOARD

Bring forth your "Deck of Sparkling Moments" and set yourself up at a work station—desk or table.

Review the moments from the deck and arrange them face up so that you may get a bird's eye view of each.

Select moments using a combination of thoughtfulness and abandon.

Lay these moments on the table in front of you in a kind of storyboard layout.

For this activity work with a total of eight selected moments.

Get the notion that you are a screenwriter who has been given this storyboard along with the assignment to create a plot and scene development that matches the storyboard.

Create such a script draft.

When done put the "Deck of Sparkling Moments" away being careful to leave the eight moments used in this activity on the top available—we will be using them in the next activity.

STORYBOARD (CONT.)

Bring forth your "Deck of Sparkling Moments" and select the top eight moments (the ones used in the previous activity).

Carefully shuffle these moments—don't bruise—into a random order.

Draw moments from the top of this small deck of eight and arrange them into a new storyboard.

Once again get the notion that you are a screenwriter who has been given this storyboard along with the assignment to create a plot and scene development that matches the storyboard.

Create such a script draft.

When done put the "Deck of Sparkling Moments" away being careful to leave the eight moments used in this activity on the top available.

Keep those moments on the top of the deck for a little while. Ideally you should repeat the shuffle and new script for a total of five scripts.

PAINT A PICTURE

Prepare a canvas with black gesso (or purchase one from our JBC Store). A 16 by 20 canvas would be best, or an 8 by 10 if you prefer. It all depends on your wall space.

Using a small brush and black paint only paint a picture. You may paint a landscape, portrait, or still-life. Make the painting as detailed as possible. You should spend a minimum of two hours on the picture.

If you stick to a standard size (such as 16 by 20), you should be able to find a nice—yet inexpensive—frame. [Author's note: an odd size canvas, such as 18 by 20, might be cheaper to buy, but when you purchase a frame you'll notice your savings melting away into higher priced framing options.]

Hang the painting and enjoy.

SELLING TOILET WATER

Obtain a half dozen or more elegant looking perfume bottles. Clean and rinse these bottles so that no odor remains. Then fill from the tank of your toilet.

Yep, that's correct. Fill the perfume bottles from the holding tank of your toilet. This is the thing that holds water until you flush. Typically it is just behind the toilet seat with a ceramic lid.

Apply elegant labels to the bottles. Something in the nature of "Undiluted genuine, guaranteed authentic toilet water."

Now find a street fair or other impromptu selling situation to off-load your newfound stock of "toilet water." A dollar or two per bottle should be a good price point.

[Editor's note: If you can't find any label material we can sell you some pre-manufactured labels from the JBC Store.]

TAKE A RIDE

This activity/experiment is designed for big city folks—that's folks living in a big city not big folks living in a city.

Get in a cab and say: "Just drive."

When the cabbie gets around to extracting a more specific destination from you ask him or her to drive away from (wherever you are) for about $5 worth of time then drive you back.

JUST VISITING

Get yourself about a dozen pair of shoes—more if you can manage.

Arrange the shoes around the house or apartment for a cocktail party, informal get together, or football party—your preference.

Serve refreshments as you wish.

You will find that as party guests shoes are not very demanding. However, the few demands they have should be considered.

HOW MUCH IS ENOUGH

Find a local "All you can eat" restaurant.

Go to the restaurant.

Have 1 carrot and 3 celery sticks. (If not available then select something along these lines.)

Pay for your meal and leave.

Don't forget to tip if that is the custom.

READ EVERY LAST WORD

This activity/experiment involves another visit to the library.

Select a book stack in the library. For the purposes of this activity we'd consider one set of shelves ceiling to floor to be a stack. This is typically about five three-foot wide shelves.

Starting on the left, open each book and read the last word. Put that book back and proceed to the next book. Do this until you have read every last word of that stack.

[Editor's note: We have seen some amazing poetry created starting from a log of these last words.]

BUY BY COLOR

This week divide your grocery shopping into four separate trips.

On one trip buy only white food.

On another trip buy only red food.

On yet another trip buy only green food.

And on a fourth trip buy only brown (and other) colored food.

[Editor's note: you may want to avoid buying turnips this week—unless they come without greens. Otherwise how can you decide? Would that be a white food or a green food. I suppose it might depend on whether or not you cooked the greens or just the root. But then again, let's just play it safe and avoid the turnips. And, by the way potatoes are not white—they are either red or brown.]

AFTERWORD &
INVITATION

Periodically someone or other will make reference to "last great unexplored territories." You'll hear that about the oceans, you'll hear that about space, you'll even hear it about remote regions of your own country. If you've performed even a fraction of the activities/experiments in this book you will undoubtedly recognize that one of the truly great unexplored territories is right here, right now, right under our collective noses.

A shift in geography is not the only way to change spaces—that you've seen. How well you recognize that and how you are able to incorporate that fact into your experience depends on your background. As with any science or art the solution to further penetration and understanding is practice, practice, & more practice. However, sciences and arts don't stop there. Another all important step is comparing notes with others involved in similar experiments. To this end we have a convention once a year. Write the publishers of this book for more information about times and places.

Dear *Just Because Club* Reader:

Since you have demonstrated the fortitude necessary to complete—or at any rate, reach the final pages of—Dr. Needham's Personal Metaphysical Fitness Trainer, we would like to offer you further sustenance and exercise along these lines of work. You may have questions or comments for us, as the publishers and proponents of this workout series.

You are welcome to contact Gateways for any of the above, or for any products mentioned in this book. We will do our best to answer your questions and supply any tools and techniques we can to help you further your own development. We add here a sample list of our other Consciousness Classics books and invite you to explore the Gateways website and the others cited below for additional contemporary ideas and practices. For a current book catalog, write to Gateways at the address shown below:

Gateways Books & Tapes
P.O. Box 370-JB
Nevada City, CA 95959-0370
Phone: (530) 477-8101
Fax: (530) 272-0184

Email: info@gatewaysbooksandtapes.com
Website: www.gatewaysbooksandtapes.com
Also check out:
www.spiritualgaming.com
www.fairgame.org
www.godd.org
www.idhhb.org
www.talkofthemonth.com

Gateways Consciousness Classics—A Partial List of Titles You Can Order

(See www.gatewaysbooksandtapes.com for complete current book list)

by Robert S. de Ropp
The Master Game: Pathways to Higher Consciousness
Self-Completion: Keys to a Meaningful Life
Warrior's Way: A Twentieth Century Odyssey

by E.J. Gold
Alchemical Sex
American Book of the Dead
The Great Adventure: Talks on Death, Dying and the Bardos
The Human Biological Machine as a Transformational Apparatus
Life in the Labyrinth
Practical Work on Self
The Hidden Work
The Seven Bodies of Man
Visions in the Stone: Journey to the Source of Hidden Knowledge
    (Intro. by Robert Anton Wilson)

by Dr. Claudio Naranjo, M.D.
Character & Neurosis: An Integrative View
The Divine Child and the Hero: Inner Meaning in Children's
    Literature
Ennea-type Structures: Self-Analysis for the Seeker
The Enneagram of Society: Healing the Soul to Heal the World

by Reb Zalman Schachter-Shalomi & Howard Schwartz
The Dream Assembly

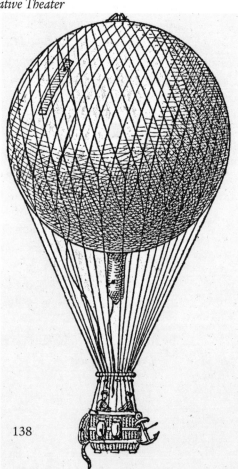

138